The
POWER
OF
EAGLES

Nature's Way
To
Individual
Accomplishment

TWYMAN L. TOWERY, Ph.D.

WESSEX HOUSE PUBLISHING
Brentwood, Tennessee

Published by Wessex House Publishing
141 Rue de Grande
Brentwood, TN 37027
(615) 370-3587
Fax: (615) 661-8944
Website: www.twymantowery.com

Library of Congress Cataloging-in-Publication Data
Towery, Twyman L.
    The power of eagles: nature's way to individual accomplishment /
Twyman L. Towery
    p.   cm.
ISBN 0-9646872-4-0 (hardcover : alk. Paper)
1. Success-Psychological aspects 2. Success in business I. Title
BF637.S8T63 1997
158-dc21

                                                                97-41429
                                                                CIP

Printed and bound in the United States of America

10 9 8 7 6 5 4 3 2 1

To my mother, Mildred Towery, who has always cared for others in their times of need.

When God made the oyster, He guaranteed his absolute economic and social security. He built the oyster a house, his shell, to shelter and protect him from his enemies . . . but when God made the eagle, He declared, "The blue sky is the limit — build your own house!" . . . The eagle, not the oyster, is the emblem of America.

ANONYMOUS

CONTENTS

PREFACE

*T*he *Power Of Eagles* is the sequel to my book *The Wisdom Of Wolves: Nature's Way To Organizational Success*. Because of the tremendous response from people all over the world, I realized that the concept of using the positive characteristics of animals as metaphors for human beings and the organizations we create had struck a receptive chord.

My original goal has been achieved. Today all types of business organizations are incorporating the principles the book contains into their management development programs. I am gratified when I am invited by these companies to present speeches or seminars. However, I was amazed to discover that many churches are also using the book as an understandable way to teach values to their congregations in sermons and presentations to Sunday school, adult, and youth groups. Perhaps most pleasing to me is the fact that families are using the book's examples to bring their members closer together.

The Wisdom Of Wolves was relatively easy for me to write, for these animals and humans share many basic characteristics. Writing *The Power Of Eagles* was more difficult, at least initially. While wolves have a well-defined social structure that revolves around the pack, eagles are primarily solitary creatures. At first, I had difficulty understanding these masters of the sky and why they have been such an important symbol throughout history. But as I talked to the people who have devoted their lives to protecting the eagle, I began to understand.

There are countless reasons why so many countries, businesses, and organizations want their image to be synonymous with the eagle. I also understand now why so many families have sculptures, paintings or photographs of eagles in their homes. The eagle is indeed powerful. It represents not necessarily what we *are* but rather what we *yearn to be*. It is my hope, in sharing the knowledge about these magnificent creatures that has been so freely given to me, that you, too, will find it inspiring and will pass it along to others.

We are once again learning to respect the eagle's right to co-exist with humans, for if we do not, the loss will be immeasurable. Simply put, if we lose the eagle, we surely will lose a part of our identity.

ACKNOWLEDGMENTS

As I entered the realm of the eagle, I looked to the experts to guide me. These are dedicated individuals whose quest is to restore this remarkable animal to its former eminence in the wild and to ensure its preservation for the generations to come. I have never met such devoted and caring people. They are well aware that they cannot achieve this worthy goal alone and need the understanding and support of people everywhere. This means that all of us, private citizens as well as organizations and corporations, must become educated and involved, and contribute our financial and political support.

The eagle is once more beginning to flourish in the wild, but without vigilant protection, this proud symbol of our national heritage could face extinction again. I have identified many of the people involved in these efforts elsewhere in this book, but want to express my gratitude to them from the outset.

Throughout this book there are quotes from schoolchildren ranging in age from seven years through their late teens. Their comments illustrate the encompassing power of the eagle as it touches the most innocent among us. Children are perceptive, and perhaps without understanding exactly why, they feel the power of the eagle to be something quite real. I thank them for sharing their insight.

I greatly appreciate the tremendous assistance I received from Native Americans who helped me understand their cultures and the close relationship they enjoy with the eagle. Their knowledge of customs and stories that have been handed down for generations is extremely interesting to me, as I believe it will be to you.

Personal friends and business acquaintances were their usual wonderful selves. I am blessed with so many of them that I will not even attempt to list them here for fear of excluding someone. They know who they are, so to all of them I say, "Thank You."

The Power Of Eagles is brought to you by all of the above. I am only the compiler of their work and knowledge.

I am the eagle;
I live in high country;
In rocky cathedrals;
That reach to the sky.
And all those who see me;
And all who believe in me;
Share in the freedom;
I feel when I fly.
Come dance with the west wind;
And touch all the mountain tops;
Sail o'er the canyons;
And up to the stars;
And reach for the heavens;
And hope for the future;
And all that we can be;
And not what we are.

"THE EAGLE AND THE HAWK"
Words by John Denver
Music by John Denver and Mike Taylor

INTRODUCTION

O vercast skies, a slight but brisk wind, the Tennessee River a stone's throw away, sweater temperature — a perfect day for college football.

And, oh yes, the crowd — 106,200 screaming fans at one of America's largest coliseums for college football, Neyland Stadium in Knoxville, Tennessee, home of the University of Tennessee Volunteers, who on this day are hosting the Fighting Irish of Notre Dame. A victory today would lift the Vols to the top of the college football rankings and virtually ensure that Tennessee will once again compete in a major bowl game, possibly even for the national championship. The stakes are high.

Soon the entire Tennessee football team will enter the stadium and run through a giant T formed by the band. This is so integral a part of the school's pageantry, so dramatic, that fans literally dream about the magic moment during the off-season. In fact, one man donated $1 million to UT, with his only request being that he be allowed to run through the T with the team. Needless to say, he got his wish.

But before the much-anticipated run through the T can begin, it's national anthem time. Professor of Music George Batzas, with the band's accompaniment, belts out the anthem in his stunning operatic voice, just as he has for years. I'm sitting on the 50-yard line with my close friend, Bo Roberts. We have observed this colorful pregame spectacle many times, but on this day we are about to witness the most dramatic moment in all our years of attending Tennessee football games.

As the band nears the conclusion of "The Star Spangled Banner," a gorgeous bald eagle is released from the top of the stadium. It soars majestically above the field, and every eye is fixed on its graceful movements. At the very moment Dr. Batzas ends the stanza, "the land of the free and the home of the brave," the eagle cups its powerful wings and comes to rest on its handler's waiting arm.

It is a moment that surpasses even the special effects of a Cecil B. DeMille or Stephen Spielberg epic. The cheering and applause from the crowd is deafening. The moment is magic, and it seems to last forever.

The Power of the Eagle!

A beautiful spring day on the inland waters of Alaska, traveling from Bellingham, Washington, to Juneau, Alaska, to a speaking engagement.

I have chosen to take the state ferry so I can get a feel for the local culture, as many Alaskans use the ferry for transportation to the lower 48. They turn out to be every bit as friendly as I have imagined. There are also many tourists and sightseers on board, and while I have rented a small berth, there are many people camped out in tents or makeshift shelters on the ship's deck. People are sunbathing, playing backgammon, cards, drinking beer, and dozing. A senior citizen tourist group is enjoying a lecture about the history and traditions of some of Alaska's Native American tribes.

I think I'm the first to see it. Floating by the ship is a large log with a stately adult bald eagle sitting atop it. He doesn't seem to be much interested in us, but are we ever interested in him! As soon as I mention the eagle's presence, the card games and backgammon sets are abandoned as people (at least the non-Alaskans) flock to my side of the ship to observe the exquisite creature, which, although it is our national symbol, few of us have ever seen. The tourists bolt from the seminar inside the main cabin and hit the deck with cameras clicking. All of this commotion for a bird sitting on a log.

The Power of the Eagle!

Sitting beside my daddy at an outdoor amphitheater in Chero-kee, North Carolina, watching the beautiful but sad pageant "Unto These Hills." I am a young boy, and this is my first time to see "real live Indians."

We've spent the last few days touring the various sights and campgrounds in the Smokies. Since Daddy is a biology teacher and self-taught naturalist, he's been educating me about the area's tremendous array of plants, trees, and animals. My dad also teaches photography, and since he has a crippled right leg, he's kept me busy carrying bags full of lenses, cameras, and film. It is years before acid rain will kill many plant species and dull the landscape. Everything is lush and vibrant.

The pageant is the culmination of our trip, and I am emo-tionally moved. Tears begin running down my face when the Cherokee are forcibly removed from their homes and herded like animals toward Oklahoma. The route they travel will be known as the Trail of Tears because of the tremendous suffer-ing and death the Cherokee endure along the way.

Although the entire spectacle is a transforming experi-ence, one part in particular is so riveting that it will never leave my memory — it is the eagle dance. Even though I don't know what it means, I know that I am witnessing an inspirational event. The costumes are dazzling, but there is much more to this dance than sheer beauty. I now understand why many

Native Americans consider the eagle dance to be a spiritual experience. It is!

The Power of the Eagle!

October 4, 1957. Sitting in the living room of my uncle Cercey's home in Huntsville, Alabama, listening to stories about my daddy.

My cousin suddenly bursts into the room, panic spreading over his face. "The Russians put a space capsule in orbit, you can see it in the sky," he yells. Everybody freezes. Then we all run outside and look above us. There it is, circling our world. How could the Russians beat *us* — the United States of America? But they have. It's called *Sputnik*.

The next day a lot of people start building bomb shelters.

* * * * *

May 25, 1961. President Kennedy is telling the world that the United States will not only go to the moon, but we'll beat the Russians getting there.

It sounds good, but can we really do it? The Russians are leading the space race. But we, as a nation, are committed.

* * * * *

July 20, 1969. Late as usual, I'm gunning my 1964 two-tone blue Plymouth Sports Fury toward a family reunion being held at a cousin's farm near Huntsville.

Arriving, I run up the creaky steps and slink through the door, embarrassed that everyone will be upset, once again, at my perennial tardiness. But no one pays any attention to me. All eyes are glued to a fuzzy, black-and-white TV set, unusual for people who work the fields all day and go to bed at 8:00 or 9:00 each night so they can milk cows at 4:00 the next morning. Finally, the same cousin, now an engineer working at Redstone Arsenal, turns to me with a huge grin and says simply:

"The *Eagle* has landed."

The Power of the Eagle!

These "snapshots" of personal experience capture the essence of how the very sight of an eagle can transform people's emotions, especially mine.

Knowledge is power, but enthusiasm pulls the switch.

IVERN BALL

No power is strong enough to be lasting if it labors under the power of fear.

CICERO

Within you lies a power greater than what lies before you.

ANONYMOUS

Man's flight through life is sustained by the power of his knowledge.

ANONYMOUS

Being powerful is like being a lady. If you have to tell people you are, you ain't.

SHOLEM ASCH

ABOUT EAGLES

ABOUT EAGLES

Throughout history civilizations have marveled at the eagle. It was so revered as a symbol of courage and power that some cultures conferred upon it the abilities of a god. It was seen as a link between earthbound humans and the ethereal. The Romans and Greeks associated the eagle with their supreme deity, Jupiter (Zeus). The eagle, with its tremendous strength, was hailed as the master of the sky, and its ability to attack was celebrated by Roman legions, which emblazoned the eagle's image on the banners they carried into battle.

Let's look at the basics of this magnificent animal:

Biology: The eagle, like all other birds, evolved from reptiles and is a member of the order Falconiformes, which includes other non-nocturnal birds of prey, such as hawks, vultures, and falcons, among others. Approximately 59 species worldwide may be defined as eagles. The two species of eagles found in North America are the bald eagle and the golden eagle.

Size: An adult bald eagle measures about 3 feet in length from tail to beak and has a wingspan ranging from $6\frac{1}{2}$ to $7\frac{1}{2}$ feet. The male is smaller than the female, usually weighing between 6 and 9 pounds versus the female's 8 to 13 pounds.

Appearance: At birth, a bald eagle's downy feathers are solid white, gradually molting to a dull brown with patches of white. By the age of four to five years, it assumes its unmistakable adult coloring — dark brown wings and underbelly and white head (not bald) and tail feathers. The bald eagle's strong, hooked beak is black at birth but gradually changes to yellow. Its eyes change from chocolate brown to yellow, with the pupil retaining its dark color. The bald eagle's feet are bright yellow and are not feathered.

Lifespan: Bald eagles are believed to live 30 years in the wild and up to 50 years in captivity. They have few natural enemies, but almost half of the bald eagles born in the wild die during their first year when they are still naive about survival techniques.

Food Sources: The bald eagle's main food source is fish, but it will also eat small rodents, rabbits, reptiles and carrion. Bald eagles will also attack waterfowl and regularly harass weaker birds such as the osprey, taking food from them whenever possible.

Habitat: Bald eagles inhabit areas near large bodies of water where there are plenty of fish to eat and tall trees in which to nest and roost. Not all eagles migrate, but most go south when cold weather causes food supplies to decline. On migration and during the winter, bald eagles seek areas with open water that offer sufficient food and evening roost sites.

Mating and Reproduction: Most eagles first breed at about five years of age and generally mate for life. Females lay one to three eggs each spring, and the incubation period is approximately 35 days. The male and female share parenting duties. For the first month after hatch, the female spends the majority of her time nurturing the eaglets while the male provides food for the family. After the first month, both parents are actively involved in raising their offspring and teaching them how to fly and to hunt for food.

Nests: The eagle builds one of the largest nests of any bird in the world. Known as an *eyrie*, the nest typically measures 5 feet in diameter during the first year and may be expanded annually until it is about 8 feet across and up to 12 feet deep, weighing more than a ton. Sticks and branches form the foundation, with the bottom of the nest typically lined with moss, bark, and other materials for softness. The bald eagle generally builds its home in the strong branches of the area's tallest tree which provides protection, more accessible flight paths, and a superior field of view.

Numbers: When European settlers first sailed to America, it is believed that more than half a million eagles ranged from Labrador to South Florida and from Baja California to Alaska, inhabiting areas near virtually every large river and countless lakes in the interior of the continent. But in the early 1900s, as America's expanding population, industry, and agriculture began to encroach on undeveloped areas, replacing wetlands and forests with subdivisions and shopping malls, the number of eagles began to decrease. Agricultural spraying with DDT caused a devastating reduction in America's bald eagle population (eagles that were not poisoned laid eggs with shells so thin they often did not hatch), and, by 1963, only 417 breeding pairs remained in the contiguous states. Bald eagles were officially declared an endangered species in 1967.

Currently, thanks to the efforts of government agencies, businesses, church and school groups, and individuals, the eagle is making a comeback. Many initiatives have been undertaken to protect the eagle's habitat and rebuild its populations in the wild. As a result, the bald eagle's status has been upgraded to "threatened," and soon it hopefully will be delisted entirely.

Today, about half of the world's 70,000 eagles live in Alaska, while British Columbia boasts about 20,000. In the southern U.S., Florida is the only state with a large bald eagle population, but through conservation practices and successful restoration programs, the species is making a slow recovery in several areas. An overview of recovery and preservation efforts, as well as a listing of organizations active in this cause, can be found in the Appendix beginning on page 153.

I am hopeful that the preceding "thumbnail sketch" will give you a better understanding of the eagle and its habits. Some of this information will be expanded upon elsewhere in this book. As we examine the eagle more closely, we will also explore the question, "What can the eagle teach us about ourselves?"

SYMBOLISM

SYMBOLISM

*I think the eagle represents courage, strength, faith, and power.
People see the eagle on coins and flags, as gods and symbols.
The eagle is more a symbol than a bird.*

— Thirteen-year-old seventh-grader

The image of the eagle is virtually everywhere — in post offices, carved into buildings, adorning the tops of flagpoles, emblazoned on billboards and aircraft, decorating the uniforms of sports teams, on Harley-Davidson motorcycles, and captured in pictures and sculptures that line the walls of offices, public buildings and homes throughout the world.

The eagle possesses so many positive characteristics that humans have long considered it a symbol of greatness and achievement. For example, Charles Lindbergh, who became a worldwide hero as the first man to make a solo flight across the Atlantic Ocean, was hailed as the "Lone Eagle" — a tribute to his bravery. Boy Scouts around the globe aspire to achieve that organization's highest honor, the rank of Eagle Scout. But the image that is perhaps most indelibly imprinted on our minds is that of the eagle on the Seal of the United States which watches over the President when he addresses the American people.

Does the symbolism ever end? No. And why should it? The eagle transcends our daily lives as it transcends all cultures and religions. Why does the eagle symbolize the very best in our society, just as it did in ancient times? There is an old Russian saying: "Striving for perfection is the surest way to kill beauty, for in real beauty there is always something wrong." I relate to this message, for it returns me to reality. But when it comes to the eagle, perfection seems to have been attained. So, what better symbol could we possibly have chosen to represent us as Americans?

What we perceive as laziness is actually competence. Inept birds waste energy searching for food; adult eagles are free to sit and conserve energy because they can secure food at will.
— Seventeen-year-old high school senior

Benjamin Franklin and the Bald Eagle

History books tell us that Benjamin Franklin opposed making the bald eagle the national symbol of the United States of America, preferring instead that the wild turkey receive the honor. In fact, Franklin was extremely passionate in speaking and writing against the eagle. But what were his complaints? First of all, he considered the eagle to be lazy and was adamant that an animal with such a slothful way of life should not set the standard for America. His second major complaint was that the eagle sometimes ate the flesh of animals already dead, being too lazy to hunt and dispatch live animals. He also contended that eagles were cowards, afraid to engage others in combat.

Was Franklin on the mark? Interestingly, the thing I admire most about eagles is their steadfast determination to conserve strength whenever possible. They flap their wings as seldom as possible, preferring to soar aloft on thermal currents at every opportunity.

The fact that eagles eat carrion is further testament to their overpowering refusal to expend energy unless absolutely necessary. When eagles do seek live prey, they tend to single out sick, injured, or frail animals. This bit of brilliance on the part of nature helps to cull out weaker animals, increasing the amount of food available for the survivors and ultimately producing a stronger species.

The eagle shows no hesitation to screech menacingly at ospreys and other birds of prey — often causing them to drop their bounty, which the eagle frequently snags in mid-air or recovers on the ground, daring anyone to challenge his ownership. The eagle is the consummate opportunist, as are all successful predators, with man topping the list.

As for the eagle being a coward, I have been unable to find anything to support Franklin's thinking. An experienced eagle plays the odds and avoids foolish situations. It attacks when height, vision, speed, surprise, and positioning all merge together to predict victory — and victory is what this skillful hunter usually achieves. The eagle is a very protective parent and will courageously defend its young against intruders large and small. Although the eagle tends to retreat from humans and our "civilization," this can hardly be viewed as cowardice; rather, it is simply shrewd behavior on the part of a wily survivor whose deadliest natural enemy is man.

Condense some daily experience into a glowing symbol and the audience is electrified.

RALPH WALDO EMERSON

A headache is a symbol that life is out of control.

VICTORIA HOUSTON

When writing is good, everything is symbolic, but symbolic writing is seldom good.

WRIGHT MORRIS

I can think of no more stirring symbol of man's humanity to man than a fire engine.

KURT VONNEGUT JR.

For years my wedding ring has done its job. It has led me not into temptation. It has reminded my husband numerous times at parties that it's time to go home. It has been a source of relief to a dinner companion. It has been a status symbol in the maternity ward.

ERMA BOMBECK

The Lone Eagle

Just before 8:00 a.m. on May 20, 1927, Charles Lindbergh and the *Spirit of St. Louis* slowly lifted into the air from Long Island's rain-sodden Roosevelt Field and turned east toward Paris. Only a week before, the famous French pilots Charles Nungesser and Francis Coli had disappeared over the Atlantic en route to New York from Paris. It was a deadly game — attempting to capture the $25,000.00 prize offered to the first aviator to fly nonstop between Paris and New York.

Armed only with a compass and primitive maps, and battling fog, icing conditions, and fatigue, Lindbergh persevered, covering the 3,600-mile distance in just over 33 and a half hours. When the brave young American hero touched down at Le Bourget Field at 10:22 p.m. on May 21, he was mobbed by thousands of cheering Parisians. News of his accomplishment was flashed around the globe, and Lindbergh soon became the most recognizable man on earth.

In 1929 Lindbergh married Anne (Spencer) Morrow, a writer, but his celebrity status made them a target for criminals. Their firstborn son, Charles, was kidnapped and brutally murdered.

In the years that followed, Lindbergh championed some political views that caused him to be the victim of much derision. But through it all, Lindbergh's patriotism was never at issue. What remains today is an image indelibly burned into the American psyche — a brave young man guiding his tiny craft through forbidding skies above an endless ocean, nobly facing a seemingly insurmountable challenge — alone. It is this symbol of adventure, this willingness to soar even when confronted with tremendous obstacles, that is the greatest legacy of Charles Lindbergh, America's "Lone Eagle."

* * * * *

The Eagle Scout

If there is a better organization than the Boy Scouts, I have yet to discover it. It has changed countless lives for the better. The ultimate rank attainable in scouting is that of Eagle Scout. I never achieved it, nor do about 97 percent of boys who join the scouting ranks. For those who do achieve this honor, it is a recognition they cherish for the rest of their lives. While writing my book *Male Code: Rules Men Live and Love By*, I interviewed dozens of men who, when asked what achievement they treasured most, proclaimed that it was becoming an Eagle Scout. Although this is a mark of individual achievement, it also signifies that the boy knew how to contribute to his community and to the community of scouting. The term Eagle Scout was chosen because it is symbolic of our national emblem and outstanding personal achievement.

Jim Hiett has been a college educator for 35 years at six

different colleges, so he has become an expert on how to interview well and prepare an effective resume. However, Jim was surprised when one college president with whom he was interviewing told him that his resume was incomplete. In fact, the president said that the most important of Jim's qualifications had been omitted — that he was an Eagle Scout. (He knew this about Jim before the interview.) Jim got the job, and the president later said he was hired primarily because he was an Eagle Scout. The president understood the courage, commitment, and physical endurance the rank signified.

The ceremony that marks the moment a boy becomes an Eagle Scout is very emotional for everyone involved. The boy has passed the most rigorous of mental and physical challenges and has become — an Eagle! If the boy's mother is alive, she pins the award on her son. If the mother is not alive, the medal is attached by the father, scoutmaster, a relative, or close friend. Jim remembers the night a young boy's mother bestowed his Tenderfoot badge (scouting's first rank) on him, and how proud she was. A few years later the same boy became an Eagle, but his mother was no longer alive. When he received his Eagle badge — now without his mother present to share his accomplishment — deep emotion swept the audience and there wasn't a dry eye in the house.

One among many — The Eagle Scout.

* * * * *

When an organization is in serious trouble — finances, employee turnover, competition, lawsuits, political infighting, etc. — smart CEOs ask for advice on how to get things moving again in a positive direction. The best strategy is to put aside the problem the boss thinks is the culprit (it may or may not be) and find out what the managers and employees are hearing and saying. It is often not the organization that is the problem — it's the CEO, and everyone else is following the CEO's lead.

For example, a hospital I worked with as a consultant for many years had for several months been on the block to be sold. During that time employee morale and confidence had plummeted while the corporate gods decided their fate. As it turned out, the hospital was not sold and management remained intact.

It had been a bitter struggle, but the turmoil was finally over. However, the CEO was mystified that his managers still drooped around with their chins dragging the floor. He asked me to interview these people confidentially to find out the problem so that he would know whether to coddle them or give them a kick in the pants. What practically every person told me was that they were depressed because the CEO continued to walk the halls with his head down, no longer speaking, and seemed totally self-consumed.

The managers reasoned that if the boss was depressed, he

must know something bad that they didn't. As a result, every-body was down in the dumps, just waiting for the terrible news to be announced and the ax to fall. But there was no ax. There was only immense negative symbolism flowing outward from the CEO to the employees. When I told him what I had learned, the CEO was shocked. He had no idea that the problem he wanted to cure lay within himself.

* * * * *

Kyle Viator is administrator of Dauterive Hospital in New Iberia, Louisiana. Each year the hospital hosts what can only be termed a Crawfish Boil Extravaganza, complete with craw-fish, beer, band, skits, and lots of dancing, laughing, and fun. Kyle can be found in the middle of it all, having as much fun as anyone else.

The same is true when we hold our management devel-opment seminars. Kyle sits around the table participating as an equal with his managers. Everyone is there to communi-cate, learn, build trust and teamwork, solidify values and pur-pose — and have fun. Kyle participates in the fun and in the work, and in doing so, he symbolically makes the positive state-ment, "I may be the boss, but I'm also one of you. I wouldn't want it any other way, because I might miss something."

Kyle is not just an observer, he is an active participant,

and the symbolic message he sends to his employees translates into positive energy, a high level of patient care, and employee happiness that is rarely encountered today.

You can think of scores of symbolic stories, if you will just put your mind to it, but the key is always to remember symbolism's power. What are some symbolic opportunities you can create?

Business

What do people visualize when they think of your organization? Is your symbolism positive or negative? And more importantly, what do you see?

Family

Words are important and, once spoken, cannot be retrieved. However, children view our actions as well as hear our words. Does your family receive consistent messages, or do your actions and your words tell different stories?

Personal

One of the mistakes of my life has been a seeming inability to express the love I feel to those closest to me. My excuse has been, "It's just the way I am" or "It's just my nature." I have finally faced the fact that my words have simply been a cop-out. I have the ability to change my behavior or I can remain stubborn forever. Do you face a similar challenge in your life?

COURAGE

COURAGE

When I hear the word "eagle," I always think that I could fly off a mountain or something.

— Ten-year-old fifth-grader

During the Civil War, soldiers in the ranks spent much of their time dreaming of the basics — parents, wives, siblings, home-cooked meals — and wondering how they had gotten themselves into such a mess. Inspiring symbols were difficult to come by, but the Eighth Wisconsin Regiment found one. As the story goes, a farmer traded a bushel of corn to a Chippewa named Chief Sky for an adult bald eagle that he then kept tethered in his barnyard as a novelty. One day, overcome with patriotic fervor, the farmer decided that this symbol of the nation should go to war. He sought out the men of the regiment's Company C and presented the eagle to them.

Naming the eagle after the president of the United States seemed only logical to the soldiers, and so it was that Abe the Eagle became the mascot of the Eighth Wisconsin — and soon became a symbol of courage to its men. The chaos and terror of battle seemed not to faze Abe; in fact, he appeared to relish the trappings of war. Standing proudly atop his perch, which bore a decorative shield of the United States, Abe would spread his powerful wings and bellow his distinctive battle cry. Abe the Eagle accompanied the Eighth Wisconsin into battle on many occasions, and his fame spread throughout the Union as well as the Confederate armies. General Ulysses S. Grant gave the bird a special salute when visiting the regiment, and once, when a stray bullet severed Abe's tether, he soared over the Confederate lines, surveying the field of conflict, then proudly returned to his perch as his men cheered wildly.

After the war Abe remained a celebrity to young and old alike, and many a famous dignitary proudly shared the stage with this remarkable symbol of freedom that had exhibited such grace and courage under fire.

* * * * *

The Screaming Eagles
Not many miles from where I live is Fort Campbell, Kentucky, home of the 101st Airborne Division. The 101st is

considered by many experts to be the world's greatest fighting machine, able to do things that no other military force in the world can match. The 101st, along with the 82nd Airborne, was created during World War II after the German army proved to the Allies that the ability to parachute into enemy territory, combining stealth, surprise, and firepower, could devastate a foe.

Their name, the "Screaming Eagles," was chosen as a tribute to the valor shown by Old Abe, the legendary Civil War eagle that rallied the Union troops as he soared overhead during battle, seeming to relish, rather than fear, the perils of combat.

Screaming Eagle training was, and is, brutal, with approximately only one out of three men successfully earning the right to call themselves Eagles. The Screaming Eagles fight like their namesake, pouncing on their prey from the sky virtually unseen, unheard and unexpected. The Eagles are feared by their enemies (the Viet Cong respected the 101st so much they would say "Watch out for the chicken man," not knowing what an eagle was).

The soldiers take great pride in the distinctive Eagle patch on their shoulder which signifies that they have reached the pinnacle of the soldiering profession and that they represent an elite organization that takes care of its own. One out of four Eagles were killed or wounded in a single month during the D-Day invasion, but they prevailed. Later in the war, the Eagles successfully repulsed the German army in America's largest military battle, the Battle of the Bulge. This battle will forever be characterized by the famous reply of the commander of the 101st, General Anthony C. McAuliffe, to a German request that the Eagles surrender. He said simply, "Nuts!" This reply immediately became a rallying point not only throughout the ranks of the Screaming Eagles but the entire Allied world. In Vietnam, the army ordered its troops to remove or tone down division patches for camouflage reasons. An exception was made for the 101st, for it was recognized that the famous eagle patch not only terrorized the enemy but also made each man a better soldier because of the tradition it represented.

The Eagles are proud of their organization's history and dare not do anything to disgrace those who have gone before them. During Desert Storm, every Eagle received a Christmas present, courtesy of their fellow Eagles who survived World War II. The bond endures.

The Power of the Eagle!

* * * * *

A young eagle that had been released into the wild by the Tennessee Wildlife Resources Agency (TWRA) was flying south from its hatchery west of Nashville. Because it had not yet mastered the art of hunting on his own, the eagle was near starvation and, as its energy waned, crashed to the ground in a farming area. A large dog saw the bird go down and immediately decided to investigate.

This was a serious mistake on the dog's part. Just as the confident canine attacked the downed bird, the eagle rolled onto its back and sank its razor-sharp talons into the dog's flesh. As the fight ensued, the eagle became increasingly excited, digging its talons deeper and deeper into its opponent's flesh. Fortunately, both the combative dog and the exhausted but courageous bird were rescued by some local farmers. Bob Hatcher, TWRA's nongame and endangered species coordinator, was contacted, and the eagle was returned to the agency for medical treatment. Unfortunately, it never recovered sufficiently to be returned to the wild.

Some people might say that the young eagle was "just doing what had to be done," rather than calling his actions courageous. But I've decided that, for me, this is exactly what courage is. We easily associate courage with battlefield situations, but we can see many examples of courage in our everyday lives: the business person who puts ethics ahead of profits, the individual who finds the strength to overcome a crippling addiction, the politician who finds the courage to vote for what he knows is right rather than for what is politically expedient, the terminally ill person whose determined fight for life serves as an inspiration to others, the inner-city youngster who perseveres against street gangs and poverty to attend college and become "somebody." The list is never-ending.

If we are embarrassed that we came up short in a certain situation, we can be sure that we will be given another opportunity to "just do what needs to be done." What "opportunities" do you have to exhibit this kind of courage in your life today?

Tell a man he is brave and you help him become so.
THOMAS CARLYLE

I count him braver who overcomes his desires than him who conquers his enemies; for the hardest victory is victory over self.
ARISTOTLE

It is easy to be brave from a safe distance.
AESOP

Living at risk is jumping off the cliff and building your wings on the way down.
RAY BRADBURY

Often the test of courage is not to die but to live.
VITTORIO ALFIERI

My father, Clarence Goodrich Towery, was one of 13 children raised on a small farm in southern Middle Tennessee in an era of outhouses, kerosene lamps, water from a well, and plowing behind mules. One day, Daddy was sitting side-saddle on a horse, carrying on a conversation with one of his brothers when a dog nipped at the horse's leg, causing it to buck. Daddy was thrown off, landing on his hip on top of a large rock. He was in great pain but didn't want to show it, so he quickly stood up and remounted his horse.

Two weeks later, as Daddy was plowing a watermelon field, his hip suddenly gave way. He collapsed and soon developed a severe infection, lost consciousness, and was consumed with fever. Daddy began having seizures and hallucinations; he was a very sick 15-year-old boy. It was 1921, and even when a doctor could be found in the Tennessee backcountry, he was almost invariably poorly trained. The doctor who finally came to see Daddy decided to "starve the illness out," so Daddy was given no food or water for several days. Finally my grandfather, moved by his son's semi-conscious pleas, decided that if young Clarence was going to die, he wasn't going to die hungry. When the family began to feed him, Daddy slowly began to regain his strength.

As a result of this incident, my father's leg was forever shortened and caused him pain for the rest of his life. He made himself a pair of crutches but was considered a "crippled invalid" by some because he could no longer do strenuous farm work. Daddy later was able to fashion a crude extension-type shoe, which enabled him to walk without his crutches, and he began to think about acquiring an education, perhaps even attending college and becoming a teacher. Daddy's family didn't place much importance on "schooling"; it was rare that anyone seriously considered attending high school, much less college. But Daddy did.

The area school only went through the eighth grade, so Daddy had to move to the nearby town of Fayetteville in order to get a high school diploma. He boarded with the McAlister family, whose two young sons, Jim and Foster, were destined to become lifelong friends of our family. Daddy went to Central High School and paid for his room and board and other living expenses by performing odd jobs. He graduated from Central — a bit older than his classmates, but he graduated.

Then Daddy set his sights on college. Instead of deterring him, his lack of money gave him great determination. He began traveling around the country as a book salesman for Rand McNally, working a year and then going to school for a year. He paid his dormitory expenses by cutting hair, a skill that would supplement his income for the rest of his life. After eight years he received his degree from what was then Middle Tennessee State Teachers College and embarked upon his dream of being a teacher.

There is no way I can ever know just how many lives my father influenced for the better, but I've met hundreds of people all over the world who recall him fondly. A man I met at The Persepolis in Iran said he never would have gone to college if Daddy hadn't given him a "kick in the pants" when he needed it. A research scientist for a pharmaceutical firm, whom I encountered during a layover at the airport in Trenton, New Jersey, told me that my father was the person who sparked her interest in science. A renowned artist confided that he discovered his talent for composition while learning photography from my dad.

Daddy survived a brush with death and faced seemingly insurmountable odds as he grew into adulthood, but the setbacks he encountered propelled him to achieve and share his gifts with others so that they, too, could succeed. Daddy had courage, and he drew upon his courage to overcome adversity. I believe we all possess courage, but we often don't recognize it in its simplest everyday forms. Courage doesn't just exist on the battlefield; it is stored in an internal reservoir that we can tap at any time. Whether we perform our jobs ethically, stand up against prejudice, risk our lives in dangerous situations, forgive someone who has injured us, or remain loyal to our spouse in times of adversity, it amounts to the same thing — courage. Courage is the stuff we all possess but must choose to be made of.

Like the wounded eagle, each of us will face adversity and pain, but can we muster the courage to "do what must be done"?

Business

Employees frequently tell me that their bosses encourage them to "step out of the box" in their thinking, but when they try to do something new, they are reprimanded if things don't work out. Regardless of what they say, the real message these bosses are sending to their employees is this: "Stay in your box!"

Family

As parents, we tend to think we must always appear confident, all-knowing, courageous, and decisive when dealing with our children. However, real courage is often just the opposite. It is being able to admit when we are wrong, don't know the answer, or even — heaven forbid! — that our child is right.

Personal

Courage means simply doing what needs to be done. But to determine what it is that needs doing requires that we have a value system. Have you developed your personal philosophy concerning religion, values, and spirituality to the point that courage doesn't require thought — it just comes naturally?

LOYALTY

LOYALTY

When I think of eagles, I think of war and loyalty.

— Eight-year-old third-grader

Unlike many other animals, eagles generally mate for life, and the eagle's loyalty extends first and completely to its mate. The seeds of eagle courtship are often sewn during the autumn migration south. On these occasions, two young eagles may meet, socialize, and share hunting territory, then rendezvous again in the spring on the trip back north.

The courtship flight of eagles, which I describe in the chapter entitled "Celebration," has been a source of wonder to humans for centuries. In fact, the courtship flight is an integral part of the mating/breeding/parenting process. No one knows why this flight takes place; perhaps it's to encourage the instinctual sexual process to begin or to reaffirm the pair's solidarity — or maybe it's simply a proclamation of freedom. Whatever the reason, the courtship flight is a deeply moving display of beauty and devotion.

The eagle has few true natural predators other than man, and until the last century it remained plentiful throughout North America and the rest of the world. The eagle's steadfast loyalty to its mate is undoubtedly a key ingredient to its success.

Leaders are leaders only as long as they have the respect and loyalty of their followers.

HANS SELYE

He has every characteristic of a dog except loyalty.

HENRY FONDA IN *THE BEST MAN*

The game is my life. It demands loyalty and responsibility, and it gives me back fulfillment and peace.

MICHAEL JORDAN

A loyal friend is worth 10,000 relatives.

EURIPIDES

Its name is public opinion. It is held in reverence. It settles everything. Some think it is the voice of God. Loyalty to petrified opinion never yet broke a chain or freed a human soul.

MARK TWAIN

Semper Fidelis (Always Faithful)
> — United States Marine Corps motto

I wasn't a Marine and don't think I was really cut out to be one. My stint in the U.S. Army Special Services (arranging golf tournaments, umpiring softball games — tough duty!) suited me. But I have always had tremendous respect for that "something special" the Marine Corps represents. And at the heart of my respect lies one simple but powerful word: loyalty.

While it is possible to build loyalty to an organization, I believe that loyalty to a person or persons must come first. Almost to a man, veterans who have engaged in fierce combat or spent time in a prisoner-of-war camp will say that the primary thing that kept them going during those terrifying times was each other. The deep sense of loyalty that had been ingrained in them during training became the common bond that kept them alive. Without it, many say they might well have given up.

The Marine credo that no wounded will be left behind is in itself a statement of supreme loyalty. Many Marines have been killed or wounded while removing fallen comrades from the field, but the legacy remains intact. Georgia Governor Zell Miller, who wrote the book *Corps Values*, believes that the values the Marine Corps teaches can give meaning and direction to the lives of millions of people who are looking for a purpose greater than themselves. He uses the example of the turtle sitting atop a fence post. One thing you know for sure is that it didn't get there by itself; someone put it there.

And so it is with all of us. Others have helped us get where we are, so the least we can do is to remember them with our loyalty.

Business

It is almost accepted as a truism that loyalty no longer exists in the workplace. Do you agree with me that human beings want and need more from their work than just a job? Can the principles taught by the Marine Corps and other elite military units be employed in the workplace, or are the two worlds simply too far apart? What can you do to help restore the human bond of loyalty in your organization?

Family

Since loyalty is a learned characteristic, how can you demonstrate it to the other members of your family so they can learn by your example, rather than rely on your words?

Personal

It is hard to be loyal to others when we are not true to our own conscience and values. Do you have a technique or guidepost to warn you when you are letting yourself down?

VISION

VISION

I want to see like the eagle does.

— Eight-year-old second-grader

"He can see like an eagle" is the greatest visual compliment we can bestow upon another human being. Vision is perhaps the eagle's most important attribute. Its eyes, set close to the front of its head, are wonderfully complex systems. The eagle sees color three-dimensionally and is able to judge both speed and distance. In fact, the eagle possesses binocular vision, which enables it to see distant objects better than almost any other animal. For example, it can spot another eagle in flight more than four miles away.

The eyes of an adult bald eagle are approximately the same size as those of a human, but its visual acuity is about eight times greater. The eagle does not see well at night and hunts only by day. It can identify a rabbit up to two miles away from a height of 1,000 feet and can scan from two to four square miles of territory while hunting. Once its prey is in sight, the eagle seems capable of calculating just how much energy it will have to expend to achieve a kill. This is one reason why the eagle is one of nature's deadliest predators, achieving success on about half of its attempts. By comparison, the wolf, an exceptional hunter in its own right, is usually successful less than 10 percent of the time.

The eagle has two sets of eyelids; the second set serves as additional protection during attacks or when it is feeding a nest of hungry eaglets armed with slashing talons and beaks. The eagle also has two sets of eyebrows that shield its eyes from intense sun glare, making it possible for the bird to stare directly toward the sun on its mid-morning hunts without danger of damage. Myth has it that when an eagle gazes at the sun, it becomes so completely filled with warmth and strength that its youth is renewed. It is this ability to fearlessly reach for the sun that has caused people through the ages to marvel at the eagle's seemingly supernatural power.

Do we humans possess a similar protective shield? People who believe they have such protection — whether it emanates from God, a guardian angel, family, friends, whatever — tend to fare better in life than those who feel they must travel through this world alone.

Keep your face to the sunshine and you cannot see the shadow.

HELEN KELLER

If the only tool you have is a hammer, you tend to see every problem a nail.

ABRAHAM MASLOW

Inspiring visions rarely (I'm tempted to say never) include numbers.

TOM PETERS

The only way to see a rainbow is to look through the rain.

ANONYMOUS

I skate to where the puck is going to be, not where it has been.

WAYNE GRETZKY

Eddie the Eagle kept our spirits high during the Winter Olympics a few years back. His thick glasses appeared to have jar bottoms for lenses and seemed the last thing someone would wear when soaring off a huge ski jump. But there Eddie was, grinning and trying and placing last — but garnering thunderous accolades from millions around the world. It was both comic relief and courage rolled into one neat package, courtesy of the United Kingdom.

Vision is no laughing matter to people today. No matter what type of group I am working with, people are anxious to know in what direction their organization is heading. Will it be sold, merged, downsized, expanded, or remain essentially the same? Will the emphasis be strictly on the bottom line, or will people development be a priority? Will employees still have a voice in organizational development, or will all "soft costs" be slashed to allow the new boss to curry favor with the corporate hierarchy?

Are we as a company going for short term profits, or are we building a foundation that should guarantee long-term success for everyone? Do we possess true vision anymore, or have we allowed ourselves to get caught up in the quick-fix mentality that most of us so despise?

It seems that fewer and fewer of the executives with whom I work feel that they have a true opportunity to manage their organization for the long term. It's not that they don't like their organization; they just aren't sure about its overriding purpose, values, direction, and long-term goals. And maybe more than anything else, executives are afraid that if short-term objectives are not met, they won't be around to find out about the long term. Most employees understand that the organization must make money, but each also wants to know: What else are we about? Is there a larger purpose, and if so, what is it? Where are we headed? What is our vision?

Is a family really any different? As adults, we often don't realize until it is too late that our children could care less whether we are corporate moguls, professional athletes, politicians, salesmen, policemen, or factory workers. The truth is that our children (and frequently our spouses) would prefer that we were ordinary human beings whose vision of family life is focused on time-tested values and spending time together. Understanding that family is more important than money and status can be the most profound vision of all.

Business

What is your long-term vision, professionally? Is it in sync with your job, or do you simply practice day-to-day survival techniques? If the latter is true, are you with the right organization?

Family

A vision that emphasizes the positive outcomes we wish for our family members equals love. Attempting to coerce family members to attain our vision for them equals control. Which of these visions prevails inside you?

Personal

Many of us have a clear vision concerning our lives, but when events knock us off our course, we tend to retreat into self-destructive behavior, saying, "What's the use?" When I voiced this feeling to a wise mentor, she told me, "When spring is arriving and flowers are sprouting, there may still be an occasional frost. But it is just that — an occasional frost. Spring is still on its way."

THE EAGLE AND NATIVE AMERICAN CULTURES

The Eagle and Native American Cultures

I like the Indians because they respect the animals.

— Seven-year-old second-grader

R ay Buckley is director of the Native American Communications Office for United Methodist Communications. He stays in close contact with Native Americans not only because it is his job, but also because it is his heritage. Much of my information about the relationship between Native Americans and the eagle comes from wisdom Ray has gleaned from tribal elders, family members, tribal pow-wows, and other resource material.

Throughout history the eagle has played a significant role in virtually all Native American cultures. Many consider the eagle to be not only a part of societal lore but also an essential part of their identity. In Plains cultures, for instance, eagle feathers were worn by warriors in the belief that doing so would enable them to share the attributes of the eagle — endurance, sharpness of vision, ferocity, and quickness.

Traditionally eagles often represented purity and served as messengers, carrying prayers to The Great Creator. A person who had the ability to "see down the road" — a good long-range planner or visionary — was said to be an "eagle person." Ray's grandfather told him that the eagle was considered sacred because it flew closest to Wakan-Tanka (The Great Mystery), the source of all power.

Today, as Native Americans struggle to maintain not only tribal sovereignty but also a distinct identity, there has been the emergence of a "Native American Spirituality." This is essentially a melding of several traditions which are celebrated when various tribes come together. In keeping with this, the eagle has subsequently taken on even greater cultural symbolism. In fact, the eagle feather has become an international symbol representative of the Native American.

As in the past, there are important rituals among various tribal cultures today that can only be accomplished with an eagle feather. Some forms of healing, life-passage ceremonies, and other key elements of Native American life all involve the use of eagle feathers. However, because of the bird's presence on the threatened species list, its feathers are difficult to obtain.

Today an eagle repository has been established at the Rocky Mountain Arsenal in Commerce City, Colorado. In fact, wildlife officials are required by federal law to send any eagle feathers or remains to the facility which makes them available to Native Americans for use in rituals. When eagle feathers have not been available for ceremonies, Native Americans have occasionally risked imprisonment to obtain them illegally, so important is the eagle to their culture and their lives.

To illustrate the great care that must be taken with eagle feathers, Ray described a visit he and his family made to the Denver March Pow-Wow several years ago. During the inter-tribal dancing, a young Northern Plains traditional dancer was wearing an eagle-wing bustle fastened to his hips. Suddenly, the bustle became untied and fell to the ground. Everything stopped. Nothing happened in the arena for an hour as five male elders were called to the dance-floor.

The elders talked among themselves. Then they talked with the dancer, and in the end decided that since the young man had not taken the necessary precautions to secure the eagle-wing bustle properly, a cleansing ceremony would have to be held for the eagle feathers. After the cleansing ritual, the feathers would remain in the possession of one of the elders for one year and then would be returned to the dancer.

From Wakan-Tanka, The Great Mystery, comes all power. Man knows that all healing plants are given by Wakan-Tanka; therefore, they are holy. So, too, is the buffalo holy, because it is the gift of Wakan-Tanka.

CHIEF FLAT IRON, OGALLALA SIOUX

The Creator also put upon Mother Earth the birds. He gave us small birds and large birds. The birds also have their duty. Their leader is the eagle. His duty is to fly high and watch over us. And the small birds have the duty to sing to us and also provide us with food.

IRVING POWLESS SR., ONONDAGA

Birds have always been important to the Indian because they go where they wish, they light where they may, and they're free. The eagle flies highest in the sky of all the birds, and so he is the nearest to the Creator and his feather is the most sacred of all. He is the highest of the animals and so belongs to all the tribes, to all the people.

BUFFALO JIM, SEMINOLE

The eagle figures prominently in many legends handed down from generation to generation in Native American cultures. The following Lakota tale is one of my favorites.

Jumping Mouse

While making a sacred journey to the Shining Mountains, Jumping Mouse gave away his most valued possessions — his eyes — to help heal those he encountered along the way. When he finally reached the top of the Shining Mountains, the mouse sat in the snow, alone and blind, as the shadows of eagles passed overhead. Everything went black. Then his vision slowly returned, and miraculously he found himself looking down on the Shining Mountains. He looked for his paws but saw instead feathers stretching out toward the sky. He was no longer a mouse. His generosity and willingness to sacrifice for others had been rewarded by his becoming a member of the highest order of animal — the eagle.

The Lakota use this story to teach spiritual values. The concepts that "touching" the lives of others and allowing them to "touch you," and "giving away" what you possess, as Jumping Mouse gave away his eyes, are key truths in both relationships and spirituality. A person develops character by "touching" and "giving away." When Jumping Mouse was a mouse, he spent his life gathering seeds and seeing only the base of the prairie grass. When he became an eagle, his vision was far-reaching and his world-view, all-encompassing. By giving away his life, he was transformed in his ability to view the world.

* * * * *

Billy Whitewolf Ford is a gifted craftsman of Eastern Cherokee descent who lives near Knoxville, Tennessee, and travels to Native American pow-wows where he sells his works of art and participates in competitive dancing. When I told Billy that I had been inspired by the eagle dance as a boy, and asked why it played such a prominent role in some Native American cultures, he told me the following story of the Cherokee people. This story is one I now share with my audiences because of the powerful lesson it teaches.

The Eagle Dance

Seven Cherokee braves left the village to hunt for food. Fate smiled on the seventh brave and he easily killed two large deer. Unable to return to the village before dark, the brave made a lean-to, cleaned and skinned the animals, and hung them from a pole for the night. Later, the hunter was awakened by a noise, and when he investigated, found an eagle pulling a piece of meat from one of the carcasses. The brave killed the eagle and then went back to sleep. He returned to the village the next day with his bounty, and that night a celebration was held to honor the hunters.

As the seven braves danced around the fire, a shadowy figure appeared behind the hunter who had killed the eagle and whispered in his ear. After hearing the message, the brave collapsed. The apparition whispered to the sixth brave, then to the fifth, and so on, until all seven braves had heard its words and fallen to the ground.

Approaching the tribal chief, who stood awestruck over the dead men, the shadowy figure said, "The first brave to fall was the one who went into the forest of the Great Creator and killed two deer — more than he needed. Then, during the night, an eagle that desperately needed food came and was taking only what he needed to live, and your brave selfishly killed him. That eagle was my brother. I have taken away all of your braves that were part of this hunt as an example, and I tell you this: Hereafter, whenever the Cherokee come together to dance or celebrate, they will remember my brother the eagle with a very special and beautiful dance. If this is not done, I assure you that great misfortune will befall your people."

From that day forward, the eagle dance has been an integral part of Cherokee custom. Common sense told the Cherokee there was a Great Creator and that He had put everything on earth they needed for a full life — plants, animals, medicine, food — everything. So, if the eagle could carry their prayers, hopes, and dreams to their God, it must be an animal to be protected and revered. Other tribes also hold the eagle in great esteem, and many still perform the eagle dance today, among them the Pueblo, Sioux, and several northwestern coastal tribes.

* * * * *

In addition to legends, there are countless real-life portrayals of the connection between Native Americans and the eagle. In their excellent book *Wisdomkeepers: Meetings with Native American Spiritual Elders* (Beyond Words Publishing, 1990), Steve Wall and Harvey Arden recount a true story told by Hoh elder Leila Fisher:

A Native American postal worker desperately wanted an eagle feather and had tried to acquire one by every means at his disposal, but to no avail. As his quest became an obsession, he began to neglect his family and friends. When he finally realized the damage his selfish pursuit was causing, he abandoned his search and invested his life with his family and friends. Some time later, as the man was walking along a road, he caught a glimpse of something falling through the air and reached out to catch it. When he opened his hands, he discovered that the object was an eagle feather.

* * * * *

Ray also shared with me one of the most powerful real-life examples of the special relationship that exists between the eagle and Native Americans. His father died in March 1991 in Denver, and on the day of the funeral a snowstorm battered the city. The church was filled with people, many of whom were Native Americans who had driven all night through the inclement weather to pay their respects. When the service was over, and before the casket was loaded into the hearse, Ray's mother insisted on greeting everyone who had attended to exchange a few quiet words and to allow them to view his father's body.

As the casket was loaded into the hearse, several of the Native Americans began pointing toward the sky. There, gliding low over the roof of the church that snowy morning in metropolitan Denver was a golden eagle. It circled over the hearse for a brief moment and then flew away. For the Native Americans who had struggled through the storm to send a friend on his journey, the message was clear: Everything was OK. God had told them so.

There are countless examples of the eagle's significance to Native American cultures, but broader society also has a perception of the eagle that goes beyond its literal essence. It should be obvious to all of us that the eagle is much more than just a bird.

Taking Flight

Taking Flight

When I think of the eagle, I always think of my dad because he's always going places.

— Eleven-year-old fifth-grader

In ideal conditions, the eagle can fly at speeds unattainable by virtually any other bird. However, in rough or cold weather, the eagle appears awkward and often must labor mightily to remain aloft. Such is the duality of the eagle. When it soars, the eagle is poetry in motion, exhibiting the beauty of a Bach aria, the panache of a hit Broadway musical, and the grace of Michael Jordan rising toward the basket.

But during a launch the eagle is almost clumsy, requiring a goodly amount of space and the expenditure of considerable energy to take off. Even after attaining basic flight, the eagle must beat its wings in a steady, purposeful cadence to remain aloft, continuing to use significant amounts of its energy reserves.

Once airborne, the eagle seeks out thermal updrafts to lift it high into the sky where it can easily soar on favorable air currents for hours. It is while soaring that the eagle assumes the appearance for which it is famous: the aerial predator hovering on powerful wings, surveying its domain with vigilant eyes. When the eagle reaches this state, it is truly in its element, and it is easy to forget its clumsy takeoff.

The same principle holds true for us humans. Often, clearing the initial hurdle is the hardest part of a task, but as our confidence grows, we can soar in our own "groove."

It's good to start at the bottom except when you are learning to swim.

ANONYMOUS

All great deeds and all great thoughts have a ridiculous beginning. Great works are often born on a street corner or in a restaurant's revolving door.

ALBERT CAMUS

The secret to getting ahead is getting started.

SALLY BERGER

In creating, the only hard thing's to begin. A grass blade's no easier to make than an oak.

JAMES RUSSELL LOWELL

One of the saddest, most embarrassing, and wasteful realities in the workplace today is the way older people are methodically discriminated against. In many industries and companies, people who reach middle age, unless they occupy the organization's highest rungs, are often considered to be "over the hill."

For example, a man I know to be an outstanding manager called me recently to tell me he was out of work. The owner had systematically looted the company, resulting in its bankruptcy and putting all of the employees out of work. My friend's children were still in college, so retirement wasn't an option. The very next day, a top executive from a company for which I had done some consulting called to ask if I could recommend someone for a position that was open. Talk about timing! My recently unemployed friend had exactly the skills and education the company wanted. Everything seemed perfect — until they learned he was in his mid-fifties. Conversation over. No job offer.

This scenario is replayed thousands of times every day throughout our country, and the victims are not loafers and unskilled oafs — they are knowledgeable, experienced, hardworking people. The idea that younger is better seems to be firmly embedded in our culture and too often carries the day.

However, an interesting phenomenon is taking place. Older (mature) people are fighting back. Armed with their experience and desire, and aided by personal computers and the Internet, many older adults are defiantly telling the corporate world, "OK, if you don't want me, I don't want you." As a result, thousands of home-based businesses are being established each year. Many of these new entrepreneurs say they have never before enjoyed working so much and, for the first time, feel that they are achieving their full potential.

Most of these resurgent individuals experienced a rough takeoff, but when they spread their wings and achieved direction over their lives, they flew like never before.

Business

Do you possess the heart and soul of an entrepreneur? If so, you thrive on trouble, difficulty, and hardship. Interestingly, your greatest troubles may come just when your dreams are coming true. Since you thrive on chaos, you may stumble when facing prosperity. Sound familiar?

Family

Human beings take flight at different times and in different ways. Becoming an electrical engineer may be the epitome of success for one person, but for someone with a different calling, such a job could be totally unsatisfying. Each family member must decide individually when to take flight and soar, and in which direction. Can you accept that?

Personal

Measuring yourself against others can be a deceptive trap. It really has nothing to do with your own potential. Will you allow yourself to enjoy the successes that flow so freely to you?

TURBULENCE AND SOARING

TURBULENCE AND SOARING

When the eagle gets into rough weather, it just soars higher than ever.

— Ten-year-old fourth-grader

The eagle is truly one of the world's engineering marvels. It is such a well-designed flying machine that aircraft designers for years have used it as a model. One of the reasons people are so captivated by eagles is their impressive size, but that appearance is somewhat of an illusion. Most of the eagle's large bones are hollow, which reduces weight and allows the bird to float if it lands on water. Its frame is covered with approximately 7,000 or more feathers, making the eagle appear significantly larger than it actually is. The eagle's relatively light weight in relation to its size enables it to fly the long hours and distances often required to obtain food and complete its migratory journeys.

Perhaps the most important factor in the eagle's ability to complete these long treks is its ability to soar. Soaring allows the eagle to cover vast distances without having to constantly flap its wings, thus conserving energy. It does this by spreading its wings and circling upward on warm air currents, known as thermals, that naturally rise from the ground. These strong currents are invisible to humans, but the eagle can skillfully locate and ride them to tremendous heights, even when there is no significant wind. From this lofty vantage point, the eagle can glide for miles while searching for prey or following its migratory route. When it needs to rise again, the eagle simply hitchhikes on another thermal updraft and repeats the process.

Turbulent winds, rather than being a hindrance, actually assist the eagle in reaching great heights and can help propel the bird to speeds of well over 100 miles per hour. Eagles actually seek out places where turbulence is produced, such as mountains or cliffs. They instinctively know that the updrafts created when a moving air mass collides with unmovable terrain will enable them to soar upward, thus turning a potential hazard into a launching pad for new and even higher flight. If the eagle can embrace turbulence and turn it to his advantage, can't we do the same thing in our own lives?

The eagle's flying skills, which enhance its ability to locate and take prey, are truly extraordinary, but it is important to realize that the "king of the sky" also appears to take great joy in the art of flying for its own sake. Eagles often glide, soar, turn, dive, and perform aerial acrobatics for sheer pleasure. This is one reason why it is so important that we maintain the world's eagle population and the freedom which it represents. While a zoo may be the best alternative for an injured eagle, it is simply not where an eagle was intended to be. After all, the word "eagle" is synonymous with "freedom."

Turbulence is life force. It is opportunity. Let's love turbulence and use it for change.

RAMSEY CLARK

A pessimist is a man with a difficulty for every solution

ANONYMOUS

The very greatest things — thoughts, discoveries, inventions — have usually been nurtured in hardship, often pondered over in sorrow, and at length established with difficulty.

SAMUEL SMILES

The best way out of a difficulty is through it.

ANONYMOUS

The greater the difficulty, the greater the glory.

CICERO

Like the eagle, we all will encounter much turbulence in our lives. The key or trick or attitude or philosophy or faith — whatever you call your belief system — is to utilize the power that is available to us. When we plummet downward toward potential catastrophe, we must remember, like an eagle in a dive, to spread our wings and allow the wind to lift us back into the sky. The right thermal will allow us to reach greater heights than ever before. If we simply allow ourselves to use the power, we will truly have the "wind beneath our wings."

Today when I speak to organizations, I use the metaphorical stories of the wolf, the eagle, the dolphin, and other parables that are not only intriguing but also provide little snippets of life instruction. There is great power in these stories, and people find creative ways to fit them into their own belief systems.

I saw the following bit of wisdom hanging on a cubicle in the financial section of a large equipment company:

"This life is a test. It is only a test. If it were the real thing, we would have been given more instructions!"

Most of us have discovered by now that this life is indeed the real thing and that we all could use more instructions. The best method I have found for both giving and receiving information is the use of metaphor. This is my technique. What is yours?

Business

Some of the most stupendous business disasters have happened to companies that seemed to have enjoyed success from the very beginning. These organizations thrived in good times but faltered when difficulties (economy, competition, litigation) arose. Their managers had not faced the type of difficulties that would prepare them for adversity. How do you help your people prepare for rocky times?

Family

Job security is a thing of the past for most people today. A family living on easy street one day can be forced out of the neighborhood overnight by corporate restructuring. Some families fall apart. Others pull together and regroup, with everyone sharing the load. What makes the difference? What can you do to prepare your family for such an occurrence?

Personal

We have all endured setbacks and disappointments. The trick is to concentrate not only on how we overcame these adversities, but also on the wisdom we received because of them. What are some of the personal victories of which you are most proud?

CELEBRATION

CELEBRATION

Daddy took me on a trip to Alaska, and I saw this gorgeous eagle looking at me, right in my eyes. Life has never been the same.

— Seven-year-old second-grader

The eagle's courtship flight is one of the most dramatic spectacles in nature. After a male and female agree to mate, their intricate aerial ballet is the culmination of the pair's union and a prelude to the act of procreation.

The ritual begins with a type of sparring as the two birds close on each other from the outer edges of their territory, each wheeling in ascending spirals. When they converge, the eagles suddenly begin to dive toward the ground. The male deftly places himself above the female, who rolls onto her back and extends her talons to the male. The male reciprocates, and the two birds lock talons and spread their wings wide, whirling downward in their mutual embrace. Just when it seems they will crash to the earth, the birds suddenly disengage and begin effortlessly flying upward again. They then return to the outer boundaries of their range and begin their unique aerobatics once again. This elaborate sky dance takes place many times throughout the eagles' courtship but abruptly ends when they begin to build the nest for the eaglets that will result from their union.

Many researchers believe this beautiful courtship ritual is actually a celebration of the life that is, as well as the lives that are to come as a result of the merger between these two masters of the sky. How do you celebrate the opportunity to share your "sky" with a partner and give the supreme gift — life — to another?

To witness two lovers is a spectacle for the gods.
JOHANN WOLFGANG VON GOETHE

It is more noble to give yourself completely to one individual than to labor diligently for the salvation of the masses.
DAG HAMMARSKJOLD

Celebration is more than a happy feeling. Celebration is an experience. It is liking others, accepting others, laughing with others.
DOUGLAS STUVA

Always remember the distinction between contribution and commitment. Take the matter of bacon and eggs. The chicken makes the contribution. The pig makes the commitment.
JOHN M. CARTER

Joy is the feeling of grinning inside.
MELBA COLGROVE

The need for celebration is deeply ingrained in our culture. We observe holidays, football victories, birthdays, anniversaries, baby's new tooth, the changing of the seasons, a new job, a raise, record earnings, signing a new client — the list of life's celebrations is endless. However, some think that we overdo in this country to the point that commemoration no longer holds much meaning for most of us, other than to do less than we should or could.

But there are types of recognition that are terribly important. When a quality team has worked for months to improve a company's distribution system and their efforts are successful, celebrate them! When a daughter overcomes surgery and speech therapy to rise to the top of her class (as my Laura did), celebrate her! When an airline ticket agent gives you a free upgrade to first class or doesn't charge you for changing your travel plans at the last minute, praise him! And when employees go the extra mile to develop a new inventory system — even if it doesn't work — laud them for exhibiting initiative, enthusiasm, and creativity. Doing so will foster further efforts that could well result in new solutions and new successes in the future.

Family and company rituals are important to observe because they illustrate continuity and affirmation of values. But perhaps the most important celebrations of all are those that are spontaneous, on-the-spot happenings that say, "You did something special and we applaud you!" or "You gave it your best, and while things didn't work out, we appreciate your effort!"

It is important to remember that celebration should not be reserved solely for victories. If we celebrate only when our team wins or our child scores an "A" on a history exam, we're missing the point. We should recognize when people try their best, go beyond what is merely required, expend great effort, or maintain a positive attitude — even when what they have attempted does not succeed. How are some of the ways you reward those around you when they try?

Regardless of the outcome, celebration is simply a wonderful way to say, "Thank you! Thank me! Thank us!"

Business

Researchers expected worker productivity to increase when office lighting levels were raised, but they were puzzled when productivity also increased when the lights were lowered. The phenomenon, known as the Hawthorne effect, wasn't caused by changing the lighting; it occurred because the employees felt that someone was paying attention to them. In what ways do you pay attention to or celebrate your co-workers?

Family

Most families celebrate as rituals the obvious things: birthdays, religious holidays, national holidays. But what about remembering the day your daughter was admitted to the National Honor Society, or your son made Phi Beta Kappa, or you and your spouse won a trip to Alaska? Family triumphs are worthy of more than one-time celebrations. How do you remember your family's hallmarks?

Personal

Without knowing you personally, I am almost certain that your good traits and positive actions outweigh the bad. Even so, I'd venture an educated guess that, like most humans, you tend to place more emphasis on the negative, but this is an emotional trap. How do you celebrate the positives in your life?

MENTORING

MENTORING

When I hear the word "eagle," it makes me want to take it in my hands and kiss it.

— Nine-year-old third-grader

Mentoring has long been an integral part of Native American culture. The following story has been handed down for generations and illustrates the importance that Native Americans place on the art of mentoring and how critical a component of individual development they consider it to be.

The Indian Boy and the Eagle Egg

A young Indian boy who had always wondered what an eagle's nest was really like slipped away from his village one day and climbed the sacred mountain to look into the golden eagle nest that was wedged into a cleft near the top. There were no eagles there, but the boy found three eggs in the nest. After making sure the parents weren't around to attack him, the boy stole one of the eggs and took it out onto the prairie where he mischievously placed it in a prairie chicken's nest that contained a clutch of eggs. When the mother prairie chicken returned, she sat on the nest and hatched the eagle egg along with her own.

The prairie chicken and her mate raised the eaglet as if it was their own. They did their best, but the strange-looking youngster never seemed to fit in with the rest of the family. It didn't run like other prairie chickens, and its beak wasn't the right shape for pecking for food. Some of the young prairie chickens, as children will do, made fun of the eaglet, and this hurt its feelings. The eaglet was surviving, but something in its heart told it there must be something more to life.

One day the eaglet saw a beautiful golden eagle soaring high above and excitedly asked what it was. "An eagle," responded the mother prairie chicken. "Eagles are the master of the sky; they are the king of birds. They are powerful, majestic, confident, and can see better than any of us. We are respectful and fearful of them, for some-

times, if we are slow, or weak, or not paying sufficient at-
tention, they will dive on us and kill us. Just knowing they
are in the universe keeps us all more cautious and alert."

Just then, the eagle began to dive, and the prairie
chickens scrambled for cover. The eaglet tried to run,
too, but it was slow and clumsy, and fell into a dusty
heap. As the large predator landed just inches away, the
eaglet began to plead for its life, saying "Oh great eagle,
I am just a poor, simple prairie chicken; please don't
hurt me!" "What?" exclaimed the eagle. "Look at your
talons, your feathers, your beak and eyes, your tremen-
dous wingspan. Do simple prairie chickens have these
things? Has it ever occurred to you that you are not a
prairie chicken?"

As the eaglet looked at its body, it shouted, "I can't
believe it — I'm an eagle! I hated all that pecking and
running around. It always felt silly to me." Suddenly, the
youngster became worried and said, "But I don't know
how to be an eagle. I don't know how to hunt and soar
and fly into the sun." "No you don't, not yet," replied
the eagle, "but that will not be the hard part for you, for
you possess all of the necessary equipment. Your great-
est challenge will be to stop thinking like a prairie chicken
and to start thinking like the eagle you are. I will be your
constant mentor and will teach you everything you need

to know. This is something I feel privileged to do, for not long ago someone stole an egg from my nest, and this is my chance to make up for that loss."

And so it was that the young eagle, with a sigh of relief, climbed onto its mother's back, and the two flew away together toward the sun.

* * * * *

Eaglets often have a difficult time learning to fly and frequently show no inclination to leave the nest. Small wonder, since for the first few months after hatching they lead pampered lives, with their parents providing for their every need. But the adults know their offspring must learn to fend for themselves, and they soon begin modeling the art of flying by repeatedly soaring around the nest, landing, and taking off again. This teaching by example continues until the eaglets have fledged (grown the feathers necessary to fly), usually by the age of three months.

When the eaglets are ready to make their first attempt at flight, they face an interesting dilemma. The continual feeding and relative inactivity of their early months in the nest have caused the eaglets to grow almost equal in size to (and sometimes larger than) their parents, but their muscles have not been trained to support them in the air. As a result, approximately half of all eaglets' maiden flights are unsuccessful, with the young birds often falling to the surface below. This is a critical time, for if an eaglet's initial flight fails, it may be injured or become entangled in vegetation, making it a prime target for other predators. True to form, the adult eagles stay very close to their offspring during their early flights to protect them if they falter.

For the first few weeks after fledging, the young eagles continue to live in the nest with their parents. The adults take the youngsters out hunting each day, but until the fledglings' stamina is developed, they usually rest nearby and watch while their parents secure food. As the young eagles grow stronger and absorb the knowledge gained from watching their parents, they begin to seek prey on their own. As a result of the adults' patient mentoring, by the time the young eagles reach the age of four to six months, they are ready to leave the nest for good. They have proven their self-sufficiency both to themselves and to the best mentors they will ever have — their parents.

A poor surgeon hurts one person at a time. A poor teacher hurts 30.

Ernest Boyer

Experience is a good teacher, but her fees are very high.

W.R. Inge

Experience is the worst teacher; it gives the test before presenting the lesson.

Vernon Law

The mediocre teacher tells. The good teacher explains. The superior teacher demonstrates. The great teacher inspires.

William Arthur Ward

Whoever cares to learn will always find a teacher.

Ben Holden

As I approached my senior year in college, a potentially life-limiting crisis hovered over me like an ominous cloud. I desperately wanted to go to graduate school, believing that it was the essential key to the kind of future I envisioned. But how? I had no money and could only afford my senior year through the stipend paid me because I had been elected student body president.

One day I happened to read that there was a shortage of academically trained people to fill administrative positions in hospitals, particularly in facilities operated by Tennessee's Department of Mental Health. To fill this void, the state had decided to send select individuals to graduate school and place them in key positions when they graduated.

I hustled over to Chattanooga's largest hospital and was able to land a summer job in the emergency room. Later, the assistant administrator, J.D. Elliot, sent a letter of introduction on my behalf to Henry Cheairs Hughes, Tennessee's Deputy Commissioner of Mental Health, a gruff man whose background and extensive experience enabled him to both educate and entertain. Mr. Hughes had a keen understanding of the art of management, including the astuteness to recognize potential in those who don't even know they possess it.

After a few months I received a letter awarding me a full scholarship to pursue a graduate degree in medical and hospital administration. I was at first in shock, then ecstatic, and then scared, for I had to sign a contract saying that I would work for the state for an amount of time equal to the time I received aid. Furthermore, if I should fail or drop out for any reason, I would be required to pay back every cent spent on me by the state.

I met with Mr. Hughes in Nashville before heading off to graduate school. He told me I was young, inexperienced, and untried — and that I would be the youngest member of a class of 14 people attending the University of Pittsburgh School of Public Health's course in medical and hospital administration. He urged me to study as if my life depended on it, to get to know my teachers personally, and to learn how to communicate clearly. He said I must always remember that, while academics are important, management is an art that must be developed, and management skill was what he expected out of me. "I have analyzed you and your background," he told me, " and you are not only going to succeed, you will excel." And I did excel, probably driven more than anything else by the fact that I believed him and could not bear the thought of letting him down.

A few years later, when Mr. Hughes assigned me to run Greene Valley Hospital and School, he told me, "You can do this job well. For one thing, you've got the ability. For another, I'll be with you all the way; you can always reach me if you need me, 24 hours a day." And with that, he handed me his home phone number. The tension left me like a covey of quail on the rise.

Over the next few years, I faced many situations that I am convinced would have overwhelmed me had I not had Mr. Hughes behind me. Although I didn't know it at the time, this was a perfect example of mentoring at its best, for he was always there to advise, correct, criticize, laugh — whatever it took to guide me into my own "art of management."

I will never forget Henry Cheairs Hughes, and I invite you to remember those who have influenced your life — and to be on the lookout for people you can help in the same way.

Business

The usual reason given by organizations for not encouraging mentoring or providing adequate training for new employees is that staffing is simply too tight and people cannot leave their own jobs long enough to tutor someone else — it is cost prohibitive. However, the turnover that results from inadequate training and mentoring costs far more than proper training and scientific job matching would have. It also is brutally damaging to the organization. What are you doing on the front end of employment to help minimize the ravages of a high turnover rate?

Family

When my family was in the formative years, I traveled too much and worried too much. It was not what I wanted; in fact, it was just the opposite. But somehow I let it happen. Have you fallen into the same trap I did?

Personal

If you want a mentor, as almost all of us do, *be one!* Do you have something to offer? Of course you do. So, when do you start?

FOUNDATION

FOUNDATION

As we make more and more technological advances, we lose more and more of the spirit we were born with. In order to live this spirit, one must live with nature; one must be free. We can say eagles are spirit because they are free.

— Fourteen-year-old eighth-grader

The nest, or eyrie, is the focal point and foundation of the eagle's activities. It is a vantage point from which to spy potential prey, a launching pad for hunting missions, a home in which to raise a family, a shelter from harsh weather, and a safe haven from predators. The term "eagle's nest" is used to describe dwellings that are located in high, hard-to-reach places, such as Adolph Hitler's infamous Bavarian retreat.

Eagles build their homes for the long term. They return to the same eyrie year after year, adding to it almost constantly, for eagles never seem to be satisfied with the status quo. If one mate dies, the survivor often prods its new companion to move into the same nest. The importance that eagles place on home and family is confirmed by the fact that some nests have reportedly been used for more than 20 years.

Jim Wigginton of the U.S. Fish and Wildlife Service says that he was not surprised when one of the first pairs of eagles the agency released into the wild returned to the very same tree that was home to the last known eagles to live in the area before the species was decimated by the effects of DDT. Many eagles now congregate in this territory during their annual winter migration.

According to Jim, eagles are very picky when building their nest and may haul in twice as much building material as they need, discarding whatever doesn't seem to fit in. Fresh green leaves are added to the nest once construction is completed. The leaves don't appear to have any utilitarian purpose but rather seem to be a flash of decoration. Some scientists believe the leaves may serve as a sign that the nest is inhabited and that intruders should stay away (no vacancy). It's as if the eagles are saying, "This is our home. We live and raise our family here. This is the "decor" with which we constantly reinforce our foundation — home."

A successful man is one who can lay a firm foundation with the bricks that others throw at him.

DAVID BRINKLEY

The foundation of morality is to have done, once and for all, with lying.

THOMAS HENRY HUXLEY

Many a friendship, long, loyal and self-sacrificing, rested at first on no thicker a foundation than a kind word.

E.W. FABER

Whoever said "marriage is a 50-50 proposition" laid the foundation for more divorce fees than any other short sentence in our language.

AUSTIN ELLIOT

Perhaps the most enjoyable part of the management seminars I conduct is when we talk about the organization's values. I ask: "What are the things you absolutely will not give up? What principles are your organization built upon? Do you still practice them? Do you even know them? Do you feel you have to cut corners to make a profit? To make your budget? To keep your job?"

An acquaintance of mine, a top business executive, stormed out of his boss's office one day. Red-faced and boiling internally, he snapped, "If he knows everything, let him make all of the decisions. What does he need me for?" In fact, the boss needed this man for many things — intelligence, experience, leadership — but he was losing him mentally, if not physically.

Leaders today need to maintain the foundation of their organization — their people — because no one is smart enough to think of everything. Everyone in an organization needs to "manage up," to initiate ideas that will help the company succeed, rather than depending on the person at the top to do so. Employees can be unbelievably creative, and they will, if we maintain and respect a strong foundation, built on solid values and management.

Isn't it the same with a family? Can one member tell everyone else what to do, when to do it, and how? Even if the person sincerely loves his family and is trying his best to do right, he cannot do so for long. Not and keep his family!

Like the eagle, shouldn't we always be adding to this foundation, making it stronger, bringing decorative greenery to it for no practical reason other than because we are proud of what we have achieved and maintained?

Business

What are the values your business is built upon? What principles are you sure your organization (and yourself) will never compromise, no matter the circumstances?

Family

Is your family really something special, or is it pretty much like all the rest that live on your street or in your apartment complex? What is the foundation upon which your family rests?

Personal

Some of us were provided better foundations for our lives than others, but the fact that you are reading this book tells me you can choose your own path from this day forward. Do you accept this challenge or prefer to be a victim?

TEAMWORK

TEAMWORK

*The mother eagle and father eagle build their nest and take
care of their young as a team. They work together and are
very successful.*

— Seventeen-year-old high school junior

While eagles are generally considered to be solitary hunters, they often engage in various types of teamwork
when necessary to achieve success. Golden and bald eagles
often hunt in pairs, and their constant teamwork and communication is apparent in many ways. For example, one eagle
will swoop closely over an intended victim or come to ground
in an attempt to flush it from its hiding place. When the prey
reveals itself, the second eagle will dive from the sky and snag
the creature with its deadly talons. Eagles have also been observed taking turns diving at a swimming duck, causing the

duck to repeatedly dive beneath the surface to avoid the attacks. By alternating their own dives, the eagle partners are able to conserve their strength. Eventually, the duck will become exhausted and one of the hunters will press home the final attack. Then the two partners will dine together, sharing their success.

Even fledgling eaglets exhibit this ability to work together for the common good. As the time approaches for them to leave the nest on their maiden flights, the eaglets begin to practice for this important event by flapping their wings to develop the strength and muscles they will need to fly. Given the size of the nest and the span of each bird's wings, which by this point in their development can reach almost seven feet, chaos would reign if they all tried to flap at the same time. Instead, the siblings take turns flapping, enabling each eaglet to get the needed exercise and practice.

An eagle's first flight is so strenuous and so potentially perilous that this shared practice time can literally mean the difference between life and death for a young bird. If the eaglet cannot become airborne and flutters to the ground or into water — or is blown from the nest by a sudden gust of wind before it is actually ready to fly — it could die unless it has sufficient strength to enable it to reach safety and make further attempts. The parents watch over their offspring during these first flights to offer assistance, encouragement, and protection from other predators.

The eaglet's preliminary exercise and training illustrates how important it is for each of us to be sure that we are prepared, both mentally and physically, before we leap out of our "nest." It also reminds us of the important lesson that we can often achieve things together that aren't possible when we work alone.

Eagles prepare for their first flights through the use of teamwork. How do we prepare for our own launches into new territory?

*If everyone swept in front of his house, the whole town
would be clean.*

POLISH PROVERB

*Snowflakes are one of nature's most fragile things, but
just look at what they can do when they stick together.*

VESTA M. KELLY

*It is better to have one person working with you than
having three people working for you.*

DWIGHT D. EISENHOWER

*No one can whistle a symphony. It takes an orchestra to
play it.*

HALFORD LUCCOCK

*Very small groups of highly skilled generalists show a
remarkable propensity to succeed.*

RAMCHANDRAN JAIKUMAR

My friend Frank Bradley, president of Notch Bradley Public Relations, believes in teamwork. He practices it and fosters it by his own example. No job is too small for Frank; I've never seen him ask anyone to do anything he wouldn't do himself.

But Frank sounds a warning. He points out that people continue to make fortunes by ballyhooing the magical qualities of teamwork. They show film clips, put up posters, line their office walls with witty sayings in frames — all in an effort to cajole employees to work as a team toward the higher good of the organization. This raises a red flag for Frank, who believes that such methods can be construed to mean "I don't have to do it." This is certainly what happens when we say something will be done by the design department, rather than specifying which designer will actually do the work. This is not teamwork — it's a way of using the team concept as a cop-out, a way of getting out of work rather than getting the job done. Frank's message is simple: "Don't let teamwork become an excuse for less individual effort."

In recent years companies have used a number of team-based strategies to produce results unattainable by someone working alone. However, it has been my experience that many of the individuals who comprise these work groups have never been taught how to be effective team members. The schools they attended, except in the case of athletic teams, rewarded individual accomplishment while ignoring the importance of working together.

In fact, we are often measured by how well we work *against* others, rather than *with* them. If we are to expect people to function as a team in the workplace, they must be taught the basics of how successful teams work. Team success should be rewarded just as aggressively as individual accomplishment.

Successful teamwork can produce a feeling of satisfaction that is almost impossible to match. It is heartening to know that, if you have a bad day, make a mistake, or are absent due to illness, there are other members of your team who are ready to lift you up — as on wings of eagles.

Business

If teamwork is so important, why do we not spend more time and effort teaching and developing it? Isn't teamwork every bit as important in the workplace as it is on a baseball team?

Family

A family works together as a team, or it is not a functional unit. This is why it is so important for a family to play together — it prepares the members for the difficulties that will eventually come. How are you preparing your family team?

Personal

The ability to be a good team player is learned. It is a choice. At first glance, a sculptor may appear to be totally independent and have no use for a team. But if we look more closely, we realize that he must have sources for his materials, outlets where his work can be sold, and, most importantly, customers. What team, or teams, are you on?

BIBLICAL VALUES AND THE EAGLE

BIBLICAL VALUES AND THE EAGLE

Everybody obeys the eagle and it is king of the sky.
— Eleven-year-old fifth-grader

O ne of the amazing things I learned when I began researching this book is that there are numerous references to
the eagle in the Bible. It is obvious that those whose writings
are contained in the Bible recognized the eagle's noble traits
— strength, courage, fidelity, power, majesty — and challenged
us to match them. The analogy between the eagle's annual
journey and subsequent return and the prodigal son is clear.

The eagle exemplifies many of the values espoused in
the Bible. For instance, eagles mate for life and remain loyal
to each other until one of the bonded pair dies. They build

their nest together, and both contribute to the subsequent additions and repairs to their home for as long as they live. They also share hunting and parenting duties.

Eagles emphasize self-sufficiency to their young, always preparing them for survival in a dangerous world. When a young eagle finally leaves the family nest, it becomes a wanderer, spending the next few years of its life exploring the horizons of its domain and flying perhaps thousands of miles over vast areas of the continent. But no matter how far it travels during this wandering phase, the eagle always remembers its roots. As the eagle enters adulthood, at the age of about five years, it generally returns to the area where it was hatched and settles into the ancient routines of eagle life — migration, courtship, mating, family.

Like the eagle, most of us raise our children to be self-sufficient, carefully trying not to imprint them with our prejudices. However, we usually secretly hope that they someday will return to live their adult lives near us, or at least to visit periodically, allowing us to share in the progression, joys, and sorrows of their lives.

They that wait upon the Lord shall renew their strength;
they shall mount up with wings as eagles; they shall run
and not be weary; and they shall walk and not faint.

ISAIAH 40:31

No one perfectly loves God who does not perfectly love
some of his creatures.

MARGUERITE DE VALOIS

O human race! Born to ascend on wings, why do ye fall
at such a little wind?

DANTE, *THE DIVINE COMEDY*

The older order changeth, yielding place to new,
And God fulfills Himself in many ways
Lest one good custom should corrupt the world.

ALFRED, LORD TENNYSON, *IDYLLS OF THE KING*

Buddy Sipe, Ph.D., is a minister and executive director of the Conference of Christians and Jews in Waco, Texas, an outstanding organization that I have had the honor to address. Buddy offers the following opinions on why the eagle is mentioned so prominently in the Bible and what we can learn from these references in our lives today:

The answer lies in the reason for everything else God placed in the Bible: revelation. God uses everything in creation to make Himself known to the crown of his creation, human beings.

The eagle was not a stranger to the areas of the earth that were inhabited by the men and women whose stories appear in the Bible. Eagles soar, dive, hunt, and raise their young today just as they did during biblical times. As we study eagles and marvel at their habits, behavior patterns, and family instincts, so did people like Obadiah, David, Jeremiah, and Jesus.

It is evident that God gave space in the Bible to the eagle to serve as an illustration, metaphor, or image to describe His own characteristics in terms that mortals could understand. One of the clearest of such illuminations is the use of the eagle as a symbol of power. The eagle has wondrous power which seems to defy natural forces that anchor human beings to the earth, and in this we can see God's power. In Christian theology, the eagle is often considered symbolic of Christ protecting His church.

Habakkuk uses the eagle to symbolize pagan aggression. Paradoxically, the eagle that protects the godly is also the eagle that inflames the pagans (Habakkuk 1:8, Jeremiah 49:16, Obadiah 4).

One of the most extensive passages that portrays the eagle is Ezekiel 17:3-10. To properly understand Ezekiel's parable, one must consider the events to which the prophet alludes. Ezekiel prophesied that Jerusalem would fall into the hands of the Babylonians, and his prediction became a fact in 586 B.C.

The eagle's ability to hover is also considered to be symbolic of God, Who is described in the Bible as "hovering upon the face of the waters." To the ancient Hebrews, a hovering eagle would serve as a reminder that God hovered nearby to guide and protect them.

The relationship between an adult eagle and its young symbolizes the way in which God looks after His children here on earth. Just as the eagle protects and provides nourishment for its family and encourages its offspring as they learn to fly, so does God protect, nourish, and encourage us.

Why is the eagle in the Bible? It is there to help human beings gain an understanding of God.

If you want to look further into the relationship between the Bible and the eagle, the following passages from the Revised Standard Version may prove helpful:

Exodus 19:4
Leviticus 11:13
Deuteronomy 14:12
Deuteronomy 28:49
Deuteronomy 32:11
2 Samuel 1:23
2 Samuel 1:23
Job 9:26
Job 39:27
Psalms 103:5

Proverbs 23:5
Proverbs 30:17
Proverbs 30:19
Jeremiah 4:13
Jeremiah 48:40
Jeremiah 49:16
Jeremiah 49:22
Ezekiel 1:10
Ezekiel 10:14
Ezekiel 17:3
Ezekiel 17:7

Daniel 4:33
Daniel 7:4
Hosea 8:1
Obadiah 1:4
Hab 1:8
Matthew 24:28
Luke 17:13
Revelation 4:7
Revelation 8:13
Revelation 12:14

THE KING OF BIRDS

THE KING OF BIRDS

Everybody obeys the eagle and it is the king of the sky.
— Eleven-year-old fifth-grader

The eagle is not the highest-flying bird (though it reaches great heights). The eagle does not fly faster than any other bird (though he reaches amazing speeds). The eagle is not the largest bird (though his great size can be spellbinding). It is king of the sky because it exudes power and majesty like no other creature in its domain. For this reason we have made the eagle the symbol of nations, warriors, spacecraft, automobiles, tribes, and countless businesses. Legends celebrate the strength, speed, and keen vision of this King of Birds.

The Reverend Richard Freeman of Fort Worth, Texas, wrote the following metaphorical story to illustrate why the eagle occupies such a lofty position:

The Fable of the American Bald Eagle

*At the beginning of time, when all the living crea-
tures had only recently been made, a dispute arose among
the birds. The disagreement was over which of them
should be crowned the king A contest was suggested to
settle the matter, but the contenders could not agree on
the terms of the contest. The parrot wanted it to be based
on running ability. The owl wanted it to be based on wisdom. The swallow wanted it to be based on acrobatics.
Then, the eagle spoke up and said, "I think that the contest should be based on flying. Flying is what a bird is
for." All the birds fluttered their wings and chirped their
agreement. And so it was decided.*

*On the day of the contest, all the birds in the world
gathered together. The signal was given and the birds
leaped into the air! Leaping is about all that the ostrich
could do. He couldn't go high at all. The parrot did a
great deal better, but all his squawking tended to use up
his energy, and he soon fell back exhausted. The great
owl circled higher and higher, yet far above him was the
swallow, whose cartwheeling, spinning, tumbling, and
darting drew the admiration of the crowd. But slowly
and powerfully, the eagle rose above him. The swallow
ceased his acrobatics to pursue the great bird, and together they raced above the clouds. Soon, the thin upper*

air took its toll on the swallow, who could not beat his small wings fast enough to gain more altitude. His strength gave out, and down he came. Spiraling even higher, the eagle rose into the sunlight. His wings were also tiring, yet he continued to climb.

The crowd below was not applauding. Indeed, awe and fascination had settled over each bird's heart. They could only watch silently and remain spellbound. The eagle had risen to almost the limit of his possibility. His wings were beginning to fail. Then, just as he was beginning to slide back from his great height, a small black speck rose above him. The birds strained their eyes. They couldn't understand what it was. Some said it looked like a bird but another bird could not have reached that great height. Only the eagle had wings strong enough to lift it that high.

"It is a bird! It's a sparrow!" exclaimed the keen-eyed hawk. "A sparrow?" queried the others. "Yes, a sparrow," replied the hawk. Then the birds understood. They had been so absorbed at the beginning of the contest that no one noticed the eagle had launched himself into the air with a small sparrow riding on his back. He had risen to that great height, bearing not only his own weight but also the weight of another. Then, as the eagle was about to fall, having done the best that he could do, he lifted the sparrow

from his back and watched as the small bird flew higher.

The birds below were choked with emotion, and then they began to cheer for their king! The eagle was their king not because he could fly — because that is what a bird is for — he was their king because he had used his strength to help another rise to heights which he never could have reached by himself.

The birds learned a great lesson that day. Those who would be the rulers among us must become as our servants. They must use their strength to improve the lives of all.

In this story the other birds were impressed with the eagle's strength and flying ability, but they really began to cheer when they understood his heart. They realized that raw strength and aerial prowess were not as important as " heart" — the eagle's commitment to the well-being of others. They understood that what they really wanted was a leader who could show compassion for his subjects, not a king who simply reveled in his own strength. That is why the eagle has endured as the symbol of highest achievement for countless civilizations throughout history.

I thought this book was finished. Then my close friend, Dr. Douglas Brooks, a Purple Heart veteran of World War II, walked into my home and reminded me that when the eagle senses the end of his life, he flies westward into the sunset. The contest is then finished and the victory is his.

EPILOGUE

One of the most pleasurable aspects about researching eagles is how accessible they are to all of us. If you want to see these beautiful creatures in their natural habitat, you can. It may take a little planning and travel, but you can do it. I have now observed eagles from Alabama to Alaska and many points in between. "Don't you get tired of just looking for big birds in the sky?" a friend asked. At first, I thought it was a goofy question, but then I realized that just a few years ago I might well have said the same thing.

But things have changed for me. Now I don't just talk about the interconnectedness of all living things, I feel it in every fiber of my body. I have been fortunate to learn about the wisdom of wolves, the power of eagles and the depth of dolphins, some of the most intelligent, exhilarating animals in our universe.

It continues to be an exciting journey for me but one I could never sustain without my readers' support. Your ideas and suggestions are always appreciated.

Thanks for being there!

Sincerely,

Towery Communications
141 Rue de Grande
Brentwood, TN 37027
Phone: 615-370-3587
Fax: 615-661-8944
E-mail: twyman@twymantowery.com

APPENDIX

APPENDIX I:

RECOVERY & PRESERVATION

It would be a gross understatement to say that we Americans have taken the bald eagle for granted. The bald eagle abounded throughout North America when the Continental Congress chose it as our national symbol in 1782, so it was unthinkable that its numbers could ever dwindle to dangerously low levels. By the middle of the 20th century, however, loss of habitat, bounties, and the deadly impact of DDT and other chemicals almost caused the extinction of this noble creature that represents our country and so many businesses and organizations.

When it became apparent that the eagle might succumb to these pressures of modern civilization, individuals, state and federal agencies, and many large corporations all joined hands to stop the carnage and begin restoring the eagle population in the wild. Their efforts have been successful, so much so that the bald eagle is no longer considered an endangered species. Because of America's burgeoning population and industrial growth, it is unlikely the eagle will ever be completely out of danger; however, its impressive comeback stands as testimony to how we can positively influence our environment when we summon the courage and determination to do what is right.

Making A Difference

Al Cecere heads up the National Foundation to Protect America's Eagles (NFPAE), located at Dollywood theme park in Pigeon Forge, Tennessee. The NFPAE has contributed much to the eagle recovery effort, and its staff works with injured eagles that cannot live in the wild anymore. Dollywood may seem an unlikely place for the nation's largest eagle exhibit (and one of the most impressive bird shows in the world), but the support of many influential people has been enlisted, including Dolly Parton herself. The NFPAE staff has nursed many beautiful eagles back to health and uses them to educate thousands of people each year about the eagle and the importance of restoring this magnificent creature in the wild.

Hacking

Hacking, a method of increasing the eagle population, has met with significant success in several states. It is based on the principle that eagles tend to return to the general area of their maiden flights to nest after they reach maturity. According to Bob Hatcher, who oversees the Tennessee Wildlife Resources Agency's hacking program (and was a great help to me in understanding the eagle), wildlife workers journey to areas where large eagle populations exist and remove nestling eaglets that are about six weeks of age. These are carefully transported (often through the generous help of such carriers as American Airlines) to areas with lower eagle populations where they are raised in artificial habitats and ultimately released. If eggs are removed from the nest rather than eaglets, the parents will usually produce another clutch of eggs during the same nesting season.

When the eaglets arrive at their new home, wildlife workers place them in specially designed "hacking boxes" — wooden structures or cages mounted on platforms, each holding three to four eaglets. The young birds receive food and water from humans, but great care is taken to disguise that fact (through the use of eagle puppets or innocuous feeding devices) so that no human imprint is received by the eagles. Such imprinting could result in an eagle growing up thinking it was a human, or being dependent on humans for food, which would obviously place it in grave danger in the wild.

The eagles leave the hacking area at about the same time and in the same way as eagles raised by their biological parents. And just as adult eagles continue to feed their young until they become self-sufficient flyers and hunters, wildlife specialists continue to feed the eagles released from hacking programs until they are able to fend for themselves, usually only necessary for a few days.

Hacking takes a great deal of coordination between many state agencies and requires considerable funding, but it is definitely helping to bring about the recovery of the eagle in many areas throughout America. But if the eagle recovery effort is to be truly successful, all of us — individuals, corporations, foundations, political leaders, educators, environmentalists, and church and school groups — must become involved.

Appendix II:

For More Information

ollowing is a partial list of organizations and publications dedicated to the recovery and preservation of the eagle:

National Foundation to Protect America's Eagles
P.O. Box 333
Pigeon Forge, TN 37868
www.eagles.org

The Eagle Nature Foundation
300 East Hickory
Apple River, IL 61001

The Eagle's Advocate
118 Briarmoor Drive
Warner Robins, GA 31088
http://members.aol.com/
EglAdvocat/sites.html

The Raptor Center
College of Veterinary Medicine
University of Minnesota
St. Paul, MN
www.raptor.cvm.umn.edu

National Audubon Society
700 Broadway
New York, NY 10003-9501
www.audubon.org

National Wildlife Federation
1400 Sixteenth Street, NW
Washington, DC 20036-2266
http://www.nwf.org/nwf/

ABOUT THE AUTHOR

Twyman L. Towery, Ph.D., FACHE, is a renowned management consultant, author, motivational speaker, and organizational management authority in both the United States and internationally. A Fellow of the American College of Healthcare Executives, he holds a B.S. degree in psychology/business, a Master's degree in medical and hospital administration, and a doctorate in organizational psychology.

Dr. Towery is president of Towery Communications, a business consulting organization headquartered in Tennessee, and divides his time between speeches, seminars, writing, and his work as a business and organizational consultant. He is also the author of *Male Code: Rules Men Live and Love By*, *The Wisdom of Wolves: Nature's Way to Organizational Success*, and *The Depth of Dolphins: Nature's Way to Intelligent Communication*.

His non-traditional management approach, with stunning audio-visuals, is effective with all types of audiences. His presentations are always customized, relaxed, humorous, and full of cutting-edge content. He presents nationwide to all types of businesses and organizations. For more information, contact:

Twyman L. Towery, Ph.D.
Towery Communications
141 Rue de Grande
Brentwood, TN 37027
Phone: 615-370-3587
Fax: 615-661-8944
E-mail: twyman@twymantowery.com